MOTHER–CHILD STORYTELLING

The Role of Maternal Storytelling in Children's Narrative Development

Debra A. Harkins

Contents

PREFACE

Every story begins somewhere, and I trace this monograph to my own early curiosity about how biology and environment shape who we become. As an undergraduate, I dove into research on handedness and how environment both neonatally (head orientation in utero) and throughout development impact one's hand preferences including how matching hand-use facilitates learning how to tie a simple knot.

During graduate school, I expanded my questions, investigating whether infants match their mothers' hand use or whether mothers unconsciously adapt to their infants. These findings convinced me that even the simplest behaviors arise from a complex dance of mutual influence, of how deeply we mirror, adapt to, and influence one another. That realization, and a narrative development course and research with a linguist, drove me to explore broader domains of development, especially how parents and children co-construct meaning through storytelling. My early projects produced studies showing how listening to maternal storytelling enhances young children's narrative skills and how parental influences, including sex differences, shape children's storytelling abilities.

Along the way, I got distracted with other academic endeavors and research and failed to publish this important research.

Becoming a parent deepened my commitment to these questions. As I watch my own child invent and share stories, I grew more fascinated with how adults' scaffold, model, and nurture narrative development. Graduate coursework and collaborative research, including projects analyzing the linguistic structure of classic children's stories like *Frog, Where are You?*, broadened my understanding of narrative as a developmental process rooted in both culture and relationship.

My doctoral dissertation, described in this monograph, and later collaborations built on these foundations. Those projects included comparing how families in East India, Northeast North America, and other cultural contexts co-construct stories and negotiate meaning. These studies demonstrated how culture shapes not only which stories we tell, but also how we tell them and whose voices are heard. Later projects examined narrative practices in Russian immigrant families in Israel and the U.S. and investigated coping styles, age and gender differences in storytelling.

Over the years, I explored parental goals and storytelling styles, psycho-social variables influencing storytelling, emotional expression in narratives, and the variations in narrative practices across clinical, cultural, and socioeconomic settings. I shared and published this work across conferences and journals as my questions and discoveries con-tinued to evolve (see Appendix J for author research).

Yet my most meaningful lessons arose from the mothers and their children in this project. Their narrative goals and styles and creativity in telling this non-worded picture book inspire me to keep asking: How do our stories take shape? Who helps us find our voice? How does storytelling connect us across cultures, generations, and times of change?

I invite you to join this inquiry. Whether a parent, teacher, clinician, researcher, or someone simply curious about the roots of narrative, I hope these pages spark your own questions and perhaps help you rediscover the stories that shaped you.

ACKNOWLEDGMENTS

I wish to thank my mentors: James Wertsch for his continual support and his truly remarkable ability to guide without pushing or pulling: Ina Uzgiris for continually serving as a model of an excellent scientist focusing equal importance on theory, method and presentation; Bernard Kaplan for his brilliant insights into the simplicity of the complex and the complexity of the simple; and George Michel for mentoring into the field of psychology. I thank my long-time colleague Joanna Gonsalves for her help in reliability coding and helpful comments and suggestions on earlier drafts; my family for supporting me in this huge endeavor and final to the parents and children who made this work possible.

INTRODUCTION

The Role of Maternal Storytelling in Children's Narrative Development

Education, Style, and Social Factors

For many children, particularly those from middle-class backgrounds, storytelling skills develop rapidly during the preschool years (Applebee, 1978; Stein & Glenn, 1979; Umiker-Sebeok, 1979; Peterson & McCabe, 1983; Kemper, 1984; Haslett, 1986; Sparks & Reese, 2013; Melzi, Schick, & Kennedy, 2011; Sperry, Sperry, & Miller, 2019; Curenton, Craig, & Flanigan, 2020). Early in this period, however, children often struggle to retell a story or recount personal events, frequently omitting essential information such as the who, where, when, and what. They may perseverate on minor details and overlook the main idea. One key avenue for acquiring narrative competence is reading stories and reminiscing with adults (McNamee, 1979; Pratt, Robins, Kerig, Cowan, & Cowan, 1989; Reese, Leyva, Sparks, & Grolnick, 2010; Fivush, 2011), which may help children improve their ability to construct coherent narratives.

This study investigated the relationship between maternal storytelling interactions and children's independent narrative competencies. We aimed to: 1) investigate how mothers and children share stories together; 2) examine the influence of societal factors, including mother's education, the narrative intent, and the child's gender, on story practice; and 3) assess the impact of mother-child storytelling on children's independent skills.

Narrative discourse that encompasses stories about what has happened in the past, what is happening now, and what will happen in the future represents a universal mode of communication (Heath, 1986). As children develop, their ability to construct and interpret narratives becomes essential for academic achievement, especially in activities that require verbal description and sequential organization.

This study examined the impact of storytelling patterns on children's narrative development. Prior to examining empirical findings, it is essential to define what constitutes a "story."

What is a Story?

The definitions of a "story" generally fall into three categories. First, the *state-event-state change model* defines a narrative as a sequence of three temporally ordered events: two static states bookending a change event (Prince, 1973). For example, *"Bobby was sad. Then he found his frog. And he was happy."* This minimalist model does not require a protagonist or intentional action. Second, the *goal-based model,* widely used in developmental research requires a protagonist who pursues a goal through purposeful actions (Mandler & Johnson, 1977, 1980; Stein & Glenn, 1979). Stories are organized into episodes, typically including a setting, initiating event, internal response, attempts, consequences, and reactions. Third, the *problem-solving model* adds a requirement for conflict or complication that must be resolved (Labov & Waletzky, 1967; deBeaugrand & Colby, 1979; van Dijk, 1980), centering narrative tension along with the protagonist's attempt to negotiate obstacles.

More recent approaches highlight two elements of storytelling: the cognitive and discursive. Bruner (1991) highlighted that stories are a fundamental aspect of how humans think, organize around intention, create action and deal with consequences, principles that resonate with goal- and problem-based models. Extending Bruner's work, Bamberg (2004) studied how narratives were constructed within context, and thus provide a flexible framework that connects structure andsocial interaction. Similary, Georgakopoulou (2007) focused on "small stories" within everyday conversation demonstrating how narratives function outside idealized event schemas.

Empirical research lends further support of the developmental significance of narrative complexity. Studies conducted by Reese and colleagues (Reese, Leyva, Sparks, & Grolnick, 2010) and Suggate et a. (2018) show that adult-child storytelling, when rich with elaboration supports a child's ability to integrate goals, motives and causal reasoning into their stories. These findings support earlier conclusions that problem-solving narratives tend to be rated as more typical by both teachers and children (Stein & Policastro, 1984), even while goal-based and more basic narratives remain widely accepted.

Function of Stories

Research on stories reveals that stories serve multiple functions and have two primary purposes. First, stories encourage cultural transmission as oral narratives convey knowledge including moral, social and practical; and narratives provide models of human behavior (Levi-Strauss, 1955; Bettelheim, 1977; Hammack, 2011). Narratives provide individuals a frame where they fit within the broader cultural and historical frameworks, shaping their collective and personal identity (Fivush & Zaman, 2014).

Second, storytelling assists in personal problem-solving by supporting individuals as they make sense of past experiences and try to integrate fragmented information into a coherent self-concept (Applebee, 1978; Brunder, 1990; McAdams, 2008; McLean & Pasupathi, 2012). This narrative construction of identity becomes especially salient during adolescence, when self-defining memories play a key role in psychosocial development (Thorne, McLean, & Lawrence, 2004).

Finally, stories provide therapeutic and developmental benefits by enabling emotional processing and psychological healing. Extending earlier research by Rogoff (1977) and Rainer (1978) studies found that expressive writing and autobiographical storytelling increased mental and physical health (Pennebaker &

Smyth, 2016). Even entertainment narratives contain embedded values supportive of identity exploration and resiliency (Stein & Policastro, 1984).

Evaluative Structure of a Story

Labov and Waletzky (1967) posited that narratives possess both a referential structure (sequence of events) and an evaluative structure (emotional and cognitive judgment). Evaluative clauses make the story more interesting and help people figure out what it means. Evaluatives can be external comments (the narrator's thoughts), intensifiers (which stress importance), comparatives (which show alternatives), and causal explanations (which explain why things happen).

Subsequent researchers augmented this approach. For instance, Bamberg and Damrad (1990) classified "evaluatives" as allusions to emotional and cognitive states, direct and indirect discourse, distancing expressions, and causal elucidations. These tactics manifest more frequently as children develop and attain narrative fluency (Zaman & Fivush, 2020; Habermas & de Silveira, 2008). Reese, Haden, and Fivush (1993) showed that when parents provide their kids with evaluative content, especially when they explain the cause and effect of things and how they feel, it helps their kids tell stories and remember things. Fivush and Nelson (2006) similarly shown that evaluative discourse aids in temporal self-location and promotes identity development through narrative.

Two evaluative forms of particular significance: meta-cognitive ("wholly external") criticism and "frame of mind" reflections on characters' interior states. Meta-cognitive comments can enhance comprehension by elucidating story structure; yet, they may hinder fluency in younger or less experienced narrators (Miller & Sperry, 2012). "Frame of mind" evaluations, on the other hand, assist to bring out turning points and make people more interested by linking feelings to actions (Stein, 1985; Stein & Trabasso, in prep). Bohanek, Marin, Fivush, and Duke (2006) additionally discovered that family narrative replete with evaluatives enhances children's emotional comprehension and aids in the formation of a cohesive self-concept.

These evaluative procedures not only improve understanding of stories, but they also help with other areas of development, such as autobiographical reasoning and social cognition.

Children's Storytelling Abilities

Research consistently indicates that young children (ages 3–5) encounter difficulties with coherence, chronological sequencing, and resolution in storytelling (Bamberg & Damrad, 1990; Haslett, 1986; Kemper, 1984; McCabe & Bliss, 2003). Even while toddlers can use and understand emotion terms in other situations, they typically leave them out of stories. This makes people wonder about their preparation for growth and the function of teaching support (Reese & Newcombe, 2007). By the ages of 6 to 7, children commence the creation of more structured narratives that include both temporal sequencing and evaluative components (Peterson & McCabe, 1983; Umiker-Sebeok, 1979; Fivush & Nelson, 2006).

Kemper (1984) discovered that young children under five incorporate merely 0–20% of the evaluative structure seen in adult narratives, whereas older children attain levels comparable to adults (80–100%). Recent research affirm that this evolution is socially facilitated: elaborative reminiscing with parents and engagement in emotionally nuanced conversations promote narrative formation and enhance self-concept (Bohanek, Marin, Fivush, & Duke, 2006; Zaman & Fivush, 2020). Nonetheless, narrative growth also mirrors overarching cultural trends; as Miller and Sperry (2012) contend, what may seem like deficiencies in narrative skills within certain populations might instead signify distinct, culturally consistent storytelling approaches.

Development of Storytelling

McNamee (1979), utilizing Vygotsky's concept of the zone of proximal development, contended that children acquire storytelling skills through facilitated dialogue. Adults assist children in focusing on significant narrative elements, progressively cultivating autonomy. Recent theorists (Rogoff,

1990; Wertsch, 1985; Uzgiris, 1989) underscore the significance of collaborative activities and shared responsibilities between children and adults as essential to development.

Bruner's scaffolding approach describes adult support while ignoring child's engagement. Rogoff's idea of directed involvement focuses on relationships between people, which makes it a more equal view. Studies show that the way adults tell stories to children changes depending on the child's age and the adult's style (Heath, 1986; Shapiro & Hudson, 1989).

Recent research (Fivush & Nelson, 2006; Reese, Leyva, Sparks, & Grolnick, 2010) emphasize the enhancement of autobiographical and narrative coherence through elaborative reminiscing between parents and children. Melzi, Schick, and Bostwick (2013) augment Rogoff's paradigm to emphasize cultural diversity in narrative scaffolding. Tessler and Nelson (1994) and Sabbagh and Callanan (1998) show that parents who talk to their kids in detail and use metacognitive speech help them write stories that are coherent and thoughtful. In general, participatory storytelling seems to be quite effective for both adults and children when involved in learning basic narrative skills.

Interactive Storytelling

Studies on joint book reading reveal how adult speech varies by child age. Mothers of younger children tend to use simplified speech and labeling strategies (Wheeler, 1983), whereas those of older children more often employ complex questioning and evaluative utterances (e.g., *Do you think the dog will get in trouble?*) (Reese, Leyva, Sparks, & Grolnick, 2010). Pellegrini and colleagues (1985a, 1985b, 1990) found that mothers adapt teaching strategies ranging from low to high cognitive demand based on their child's verbal competence, and that higher-demand strategies (such as cause-effect reasoning and evaluative questions) correlate with more advanced storytelling. Haden, Haight, and Elischberger (2009) stressed the significance of causal and evaluative prompts in helping children's understanding and self-expression.

Demir et al. (2015) investigated parental use of mental state language and causal speech within narrative interactions, predicting children's subsequent narrative competency. These results align with previous studies demonstrating that high-quality, interactive language experiences, especially those abundant in narrative scaffolding, are essential for academic readiness and story comprehension (Skarakis-Doyle & Dempsey, 2008; Zauche, Thul, Mahoney, & Stapel-Wax, 2016).

Present Research

This study analyzed mother-child storytelling patterns and their correlation with children's independent storytelling skills. Based on previous studies, I put forward the following hypotheses:

1. The level of interactivity during storytelling would differ among mother-child dyads.
2. More engaged storytelling patterns would be linked to more educated mothers.
3. The goals mothers have for their stories would be related to their education levels and the sorts of stories they tell.
4. More participatory storytelling patterns would lead to better narrative performance in children's independent storytelling.

A small preliminary study indicated that older preschoolers (ages 4–5) participated in more involved storytelling with their parents and exhibited superior narrative recall compared to their younger counterparts. We needed a larger study to distinguish possible age effects from maternal storytelling goals and styles.

We investigated the correlation between the number and kind of maternal inquiries and responses during collaborative storytelling and a child's ability to independently narrate a story. We also examined how maternal intentions, education, and the child's gender influenced this process.

METHOD

Participants

Thirty-six English-speaking mothers and their four- to five-year-old children (M = 4.9 years, SD = 5 months) participated in the study. The sample included 19 females (M = 4.10 years, SD = 6 months) and 17 males (M = 4.8 years, SD = 3 months), all from middle-class backgrounds.

Materials

The wordless picture book *Frog, Where Are You?* by Mercer Mayer was selected for three reasons: (1) its lack of text ensures that all narration is generated by the reader, allowing researchers to observe children's spontaneous narrative production without textual scaffolding (Paris & Paris, 2003; Curenton & Craig, 2011); (2) its episodic and goal structure have been extensively analyzed in narrative research, making it a well-established tool for assessing story schema and causal reasoning (Bamberg, 1987; Bamberg & Marchman, 1991; Trabasso, in prep; Lindholm & Dockrell, 2012); and (3) prior studies have examined how narrators use internal state evaluatives in retellings of this specific story, offering a comparative framework for analyzing emotional and cognitive commentary (Bamberg & Damrad, 1990; Demir, Levine, & Goldin-Meadow, 2015; Reese & Newcombe, 2007).

Procedure

On Day 1, we instructed mothers (see Appendix A) to engage in a naturalistic storytelling session with their child using the picture book. We audio recorded the storytelling in the families' homes. On

Day 3, we asked children to retell the story independently to the experimenter. If necessary, we used prompts (Appendix B) to elicit storytelling. Parents also completed a questionnaire (Appendix C) on their storytelling goals, education, and practices.

Measures

Story length: We analyzed count phrases (subject-verb units) produced by mothers and children.

Maternal questions: Six mutually exclusive question types were coded (Table 1): (1) labeling (e.g., "*Who is this?*"); (2) yes/no; (3) tag (e.g., "*He's looking in the hole, isn't he?*"); (4) text-to-life links; (5) descriptive-event (e.g., "*What happened?*"); and (6) evaluative (e.g., "*Why do you think he is looking over the log?*"). Interrater reliability (kappa) = .89.

Table 1
Frequency (SD) of Mothers' Questions during Mother-Child Storytelling

Type of Question	N of Dyads	Proportion of Dyads	Mean Frequency	SD
Tag Questions	16	0.44	1.58	2.17
Yes/No Questions	21	0.58	2.10	1.18
Labeling Questions	29	0.81	5.75	5.04
Descriptive Questions	30	0.83	8.97	8.65

Evaluative comments: Evaluatives were coded as (a) internal frame of mind references, (b) character speech, (c) goal-related statements, or (d) meta-cognitive comments (See Table 2). Their location in the narrative was also noted. Interrater reliability = .86.

Table 2
Frequency (SD) of Mothers' Evaluative Use During Mother-Child Storytelling

Type of Evaluative	Mean Frequency	SD
Frame of Mind	6.58	6.45
Character Speech	4.69	4.49
Goal-Related	13.11	6.45
Meta-Cognitive	15.39	13.14

Storytelling patterns: Child responses to parental prompts were categorized as labeling, verifying, confirming, narrating, explaining, anticipating, or relating personal experience (rare; excluded from analysis) (See Table 3). Interrater reliability = .85.

Storytelling patterns were grouped into three categories: (1) explanatory storytelling (child explains motives/causes), (2) narrative-focused storytelling (child narrates events without explaining causes), and (3) low-interactivity storytelling.

Table 3

Frequency (SD) of Children's Responses to Mothers' Questions During Mother-Child Storytelling

Response Type	n	Proportion	Mean	SD
Label	36	.88	6.28	4.63
Verify/Confirming	29	.81	5.93	4.83
Narrate Story Event	24	.67	10.36	10.84
Motive/Cause	13	.36	1.16	1.36
Personal Experience	2	.06	0.25	0.55

Maternal strategies: Parents' reported storytelling preferences (e.g., uninterrupted reading, asking comprehension questions, frequent discussion) and goals (e.g., comprehension, bonding, school readiness, enjoyment) were compared to actual behavior and child performance.

Children's narrative performance: Independent narratives were coded for structural elements (setting, initiating event, internal response, attempt, consequence, reaction) and deviations from prototypic narrative structure (Mandler & Johnson, 1977; Stein & Policastro, 1984). Interrater reliability = .88.

RESULTS/DISCUSSION

This study aimed to investigate the relationship between mother-child storytelling styles and children's independent narrative performance. This required analysis of the storytelling strategies used by mothers and children during storybook reading, examination of social factors (such as mothers' educational levels, reading goals, and child gender), and assessment of children's independent storytelling abilities.

Mother-child storytelling patterns

Initial analyses of the "frog" storybook sessions revealed significant variability across dyads in terms of narrative length (ranging from 50 to 220 phrases), number of questions asked by mothers (0 to 101), and number of child utterances (0 to 127). The types and frequencies of maternal questions also varied widely. While child-initiated questions were rare, mothers asked several types, including: (1) labeling (e.g., "*Who went to bed?*"); (2) yes/no (e.g., "*Is that a dog?*"); (3) tag (e.g., "*He's looking in the hole, isn't he?*"); (4) personal experience (e.g., "*Do you remember when you found a bee's nest?*"); (5) event-describing (e.g., "*What happened next?*"); and (6) evaluative questions (e.g., "*Why is he looking for the frog?*").

A MANOVA testing for variation in question types revealed a significant effect, Hotelling's $F = 11.62$, $p < .001$. Post-hoc comparisons showed that mothers asked significantly more evaluative than labeling questions ($F = 6.69$, $p < .05$), more descriptive than yes/no questions ($F = 13.99$, $p < .01$), and more labeling than tag questions ($F = 4.3$, $p < .05$), though not more than yes/no questions. Evaluative questions appeared in 83% of the narratives, followed by event-describing and labeling/verifying (81%), yes/no (58%), tag (44%), and personal experience (8%) questions.

These findings suggest that mothers commonly employed questioning strategies designed to elicit children's active narration and evaluation of story events. This aligns with earlier research (Haslett, 1985; Kemper, 1984; Peterson & McCabe, 1983), which showed that children aged 4–5 often struggle to include evaluative content in their own narratives.

To examine the types of evaluation used, researchers coded mothers' evaluative utterances as: (1) frame of mind (inferring characters' thoughts or feelings); (2) character speech (imagining what a character says); (3) goal (referring to the objective of the story); and (4) meta-cognitive (providing or prompting commentary from the narrator's or listener's perspective).

A MANOVA found significant variation in evaluative use, Hotelling's $F = 22.68$, $p < .001$. Mothers used significantly more meta-cognitive evaluatives than either character speech ($F = 7.73$, $p < .01$) or frame of mind ($F = 6.36$, $p < .05$), though not more than goal-related evaluatives. Goal-related evaluatives also outnumbered character speech ($F = 6.08$, $p < .05$) and frame of mind ($F = 4.71$, $p < .05$). There was no difference between the latter two.

Most mothers (90%) employed each type of evaluative at least once, though frequencies varied: frame of mind (range = 0–39), character speech (0–21), goal-related (0–26), and meta-cognitive (0–49). This variability underscores the diversity of maternal storytelling approaches.

Meta-cognitive evaluatives were often embedded in questions (e.g., "Why do you think he looks happy?"), supported by a strong positive correlation between meta-cognitive evaluatives and total maternal questions, $r(34) = .64$, $p < .001$. In contrast, the use of character speech and goal-related evaluatives was negatively correlated with total questions, $r(34) = -.45$, $p < .01$ and $r(34) = -.37$, $p < .05$, respectively (See Table 4).

Table 4

Frequency (SD) of Children's Evaluative Use During Mother-Child Storytelling

Evaluative Type	Mean	SD
Frame of Mind	1.22	1.59
Character Speech	1.39	2.03
Goal–Related	3.67	3.27
Meta–Cognitive	3.67	5.55

These findings suggest that meta–cognitive evaluatives tend to co-occur with interactive storytelling patterns that encourage child participation. Conversely, storytelling dominated by character speech or goal-related commentary may be more monologic, possibly limiting child engagement.

Child participation during storybook reading

Children's utterances also varied greatly in both frequency and type. Notably, 95% of children's speech occurred in response to mothers' questions. Children's responses were categorized as: (1) labeling (e.g., M:*"Who is that?"* C:*"Doggy"*); (2) verifying or confirming (M:*"Is that a dog?"* C:*"No"*); (3) narrating story events (M:*"What happened next?"* C:*"He jumped out."*); (4) explaining motives or causes (M:*"Why does the boy look like that?"* C:*"Because he broke the jar."*); and (5) relating personal experiences (M:*"Do the bees sting him?"* C:*"Bees try to bite me."*).

A MANOVA revealed a significant effect of response type, Hotelling's $F = 19.59$, $p < .001$. Post-hoc comparisons showed that children provided significantly more story event narrations than labeling ($F = 7.34$, $p < .01$), verifying ($F = 7.89$, $p < .01$), or explanatory ($F = 21.85$, $p < .01$) responses. Labeling responses exceeded explanatory responses ($F = 7.66$, $p < .01$), as did verifying responses ($F = 6.25$, $p < .05$). There was no significant difference between labeling and verifying responses.

Thus, while children were most likely to narrate story events, they were much less likely to explain motives or causes, despite mothers' frequent use of evaluative questions. Only 14 children (39% of the sample) gave responses that included explanations for characters' behaviors—designated here as the "motive/cause" group.

A representative dialogue from this group:

M: "What do you think happened here?"

C: "He's gone."

M: "Yeah, does he look happy or sad?"

C: "Sad."

M: "Why do you think he's sad?"

C: "Because he lost his frog."

In this exchange, the child narrates the event, labels an emotion, and explains its cause—demonstrating evaluative depth. Children were grouped into three storytelling styles: (1) motive/cause group (explained story motives), (2) story event group (narrated events only), and (3) non-interactive group (minimal responses).

A 4 (evaluative type) × 3 (storytelling style) mixed ANOVA showed main effects for evaluative type, $F(3,132) = 4.33, p < .01$, and storytelling style, $F(2,132) = 8.64, p < .001$. Post-hoc tests revealed that children used significantly more meta-cognitive evaluatives than frame of mind ($F = 4.24, p < .05$) or character speech ($F = 3.95, p < .05$), and more goal-related evaluatives than either of those two.

Children in the motive/cause group used significantly more evaluation than those in the story event group ($F = 5.88, p < .05$), who in turn used more than those in the non-interactive group ($F = 6.24, p < .05$). Children in the motive/cause group also outperformed the non-interactive group significantly ($F = 11.26, p < .01$).

These results suggest that some children are indeed capable of evaluative storytelling at this age, especially when prompted. However, individual differences in maternal prompting may influence whether these capabilities are expressed. It is possible that children in the non-interactive or story-event groups had the potential to provide evaluative commentary but were not given the opportunity to do so by their mothers' questioning strategies.

Mother-child storybook readings in which children narrated events without explaining the motives or causes behind them—comprising 39% of the narratives—were analyzed to determine whether mothers posed questions that might have prompted such explanatory responses. The excerpt below typifies this "story-event" group:

M: "Oops, it looks like the little boy was woken up—what has he found?"

C: "No frog."

M: "Oh, he must be very sad, don't you think?"

M: "Just looking, saying: 'Oh no, my froggy's gone.'"

In this interaction, the mother prompts the child to describe the event, and the child does so. The mother then offers a tag question to label the emotion but does not explicitly ask for a motive or cause. Instead, she provides the evaluation herself. As a result, it remains unclear whether the child might have been capable of explaining the event's cause if prompted.

For the remaining children classified as the "non-interactive" group it is uncertain whether their lack of explanatory or narrative responses stemmed from limited ability or from a lack of prompting. This group was marked by low maternal questioning, often limited to yes/no, labeling, or tag questions. Four mothers in this group asked no questions at all. When questions were posed, they rarely invited extended narrative or evaluation. A representative example follows:

M: "Do you think it's daytime or nighttime?" C: "Nighttime."

One plausible explanation is that some mothers avoided open-ended questions due to assumptions about their child's ability to respond. Still, a few mothers in this group attempted to elicit narration, as in the following exchange:

M: "What happened?" [pause]
M: "What happened here?" [pause]

M: "What happened to the jar?" [pause]
M: "It broke, huh?" [pause]
M: "Do you think the dog got hurt?" [pause]
M: "Does the boy look happy?" [pause]
M: "No, he doesn't look happy, does he?"

C: "No."

Here, the mother progressively simplifies her questions yet receives only minimal response. This illustrates how the child's limited participation shaped the mother's narrative dominance. Overall, most mothers in this group asked few questions and elicited limited child input.

These findings suggest the existence of three storytelling styles associated with varying levels of child engagement: (1) children narrating and explaining story events; (2) children narrating without explaining motives; and (3) children responding minimally, often with yes/no or labeling responses.

It is possible that mothers adapted their questioning styles based on their perceptions of their child's abilities. Consequently, some children may have had more opportunities to practice narration and evaluation, potentially reinforcing emerging skills. While this study does not investigate how such abilities develop, the findings suggest that certain children contribute meaningful narrative structure during shared storytelling. Others, particularly those in the non-interactive group, may have similar potential but lack the opportunity to express it. Differences across these groups may also relate to other variables, such as child gender or maternal education, which will be explored in subsequent sections.

These findings also align with storytelling classifications from prior research. Pellegrini et al. (1990) and Dickinson & Keebler (1989) described joint storytelling styles that varied in cognitive demand. Pellegrini observed that mothers adjusted their strategies based on children's competence, measured through vocabulary tests. In contrast, the current study's higher levels of child participation enabled a more direct analysis of how maternal strategies related to children's narrative responses.

The three storytelling styles identified here, motive/cause, story-event, and non-interactive, correspond loosely to Pellegrini's classifications of high, medium, and low mental demand, respectively (See Table 5). Mothers in the non-interactive group resemble those in Pellegrini's low-demand group, using labeling and tag questions with minimal evaluative depth. The story-event group parallels Pellegrini's medium-demand strategy, emphasizing sequencing and clarification. Finally, mothers in the motive/cause group mirrored high-demand strategies by prompting evaluations, inferences, and narrative conclusions.

Table 5

Frequency (SD) of Children's Evaluative Use According to Mother-Child Storytelling Pattern

Storytelling Pattern	Mean	SD
Non-interactive	2.88	2.85
Story Event	9.36	6.81
Motive/Cause	14.57	13.69

In summary, distinct mother-child storytelling styles emerged, each associated with different levels of child participation. These styles appear to reflect both maternal goals and children's narrative abilities. In the next section, we turn to the social factors—such as maternal education, child gender, and maternal goals—that may influence these patterns.

Mothers' Educational Level and Storytelling Pattern

A notable difference between this study and that of Pellegrini et al. (1990) lies in both children's narrative participation and socio-economic background. While the Pellegrini study involved Black Head Start children and their mothers, participants in the present study were predominantly middle and upper-middle class. The average maternal education in the Pellegrini sample was 10.92 years, compared to 13.9 years in the current study. Additionally, Pellegrini used worded storybooks, whereas this study employed a wordless book, a methodological difference to be addressed later. Prior research has also linked economic class with differences in storytelling styles (Ninio, 1980).

Given these contextual differences, maternal education emerged as a possible factor influencing storytelling patterns. An analysis of variance revealed a significant condition effect, $F(2, 26) = 4.12$, $p < .05$. Post-hoc comparisons using Tukey's method indicated that mothers with more than four years of college were significantly more likely to engage in story-event-focused and motive/cause-focused storytelling. In contrast, mothers with four years of college or less tended to adopt a non-interactive storytelling pattern.

These findings suggest that maternal education may play a key role in shaping how mothers engage their children during shared reading experiences.

Mothers' Educational Level, Child Gender, and Storytelling Style

Further analyses examined how maternal education and child gender jointly influenced storytelling strategies, particularly the types and frequency of maternal questions. A MANOVA revealed a significant interaction between gender and education, Hotelling's $F = 3.4$, $p < .028$. Post-hoc results showed that mothers with more education asked more story-event questions to sons ($M = 16.2$, $SD = 9.65$) than to daughters ($M = 6.83$, $SD = 5.98$), while mothers with less education asked more such questions to daughters ($M = 9.25$, $SD = 8.92$) than to sons ($M = 3.17$, $SD = 3.37$), $F(1, 20) = 11.12$, $p < .003$.

Evaluative use by both mothers and children was also examined. A MANOVA showed a significant main effect of maternal education, Hotelling's $F = 2.79$, $p < .03$. Post-hoc tests revealed that mothers with more education used significantly fewer instances of character speech ($F(1, 26) = 4.08$, $p < .05$) and goal-related evaluatives ($F(1, 26) = 14.04$, $p < .001$). In contrast, their children used significantly more frame-of-mind ($F(1, 26) = 4.81$, $p < .037$) and character speech evaluatives ($F(1, 26) = 6.7$, $p < .016$) than children whose mothers had less education (see Table). No other effects were statistically significant.

Table 86

Frequency (SD) of Mother and Child Evaluative-Use According to Mothers' Educational Level

Type of Evaluative	< 16 Years of Schooling	> 16 Years of Schooling	F
Mother			
Character Speech	7.71 (8.21)	3.69 (2.47)	4.08 ★
Goal-related	18.00 (7.78)	11.19 (6.35)	14.04 ★★★
Child			
Frame of Mind	1.71 (2.76)	3.31 (2.70)	4.81 ★
Character Speech	1.14 (2.35)	3.94 (3.28)	6.70 ★★

★ *p < .05*
★★ *p < .02*
★★★ *p < .001*

These results suggest that mothers with different educational backgrounds may hold different intentions when engaging in shared reading. To explore this, mothers were asked to select the primary goal of storytelling: (a) social enjoyment (e.g., fostering a love of books and shared time), or (b) comprehension (e.g., preparing the child for school or enhancing reading readiness). A Fisher exact test revealed that mothers with more education more frequently selected "social enjoyment," while those with less education chose "comprehension" as their primary goal (p < .01). No significant relationship was found between maternal education, reported goal of storytelling, and child gender.

Reported Goals and Reading Preferences

Analyses also examined whether mothers' stated goals corresponded with their reported reading styles. A Spearman rank-order correlation showed a strong association between goal and style, rs(32) = .97, p < .00. Mothers aiming for comprehension or school preparation preferred uninterrupted reading or occasional pauses. In contrast, those prioritizing social enjoyment favored frequent pauses to ask questions and discuss the story.

These findings highlight two distinct approaches. Mothers emphasizing comprehension often adopted a more directive style, assuming that uninterrupted narration would optimize understanding. Child questions or interruptions may be viewed as distractions. This approach may reflect an effort to simulate a school-like listening environment.

Conversely, mothers focused on enjoyment encouraged interaction, posing frequent questions and inviting their children into the storytelling process. Although not aimed explicitly at comprehension, this method may nonetheless support deeper narrative engagement and understanding through active participation (See Table 7 and 8).

Table 7

Frequency (SD) of Mothers' Questions According to Mother-Child Storytelling Pattern

Type of Question	Non-interactive	Story Event	Motive/Cause
n	8	14	14
Labeling	2.38 (4.24)	4.86 (4.19)	5.71 (2.76)
Tag	0.50 (1.07)	2.21 (2.29)	1.78 (2.33)
Yes/No	2.00 (3.42)	3.57 (2.82)	4.29 (4.83)
Descriptive	1.75 (2.31)	9.28 (7.06)	12.71 (10.11)
Evaluative	2.63 (3.50)	6.36 (5.09)	12.79 (11.30)
Personal Experience	0.12 (0.35)	---------	0.43 (1.16)

Table 8

Children's Responses to Mothers' Questions During Mother-Child Storytelling

Types of Responses	Non-interactive	Story Event	Motive/Cause
n	8	14	14
Labeling	2.00 (3.07)	6.86 (4.26)	7.07 (3.69)
Verify/Confirm	1.63 (2.77)	4.00 (3.24)	7.29 (5.66)
Descriptive	1.63 (1.56)	9.85 (3.67)	16.00 (14.26)
Evaluative	-----	-------	2.21 (1.42)
Personal Experience	0.25 (0.46)	0.14 (0.36)	0.36 (0.74)
Total	5.88 (7.08)	21.42 (11.25)	33.21 (17.07)

Together, these analyses suggest that maternal goals shaped in part by educational background are closely tied to both storytelling style and the nature of mother–child interaction during shared reading.

Mothers' Goals and Actual Storytelling Behavior

To determine whether reported goals and styles corresponded with actual behavior during storytelling, additional analyses were conducted. Mothers who reported preferring to "stop frequently and discuss the story" told significantly longer stories (M = 158 phrases, SD = 68) than those who preferred to "read uninterrupted" (M = 102 phrases, SD = 41), t(32) = 2.42, p < .05. Likewise, children of mothers reporting social enjoyment as their goal were more verbally active (M = 28.74 phrases, SD = 10.18) than those whose mothers prioritized comprehension (M = 19.86 phrases, SD = 10.57), t(32) = 2.04, p < .05 (see Table 9).

Table 9

Mothers' Reported Goals of Storytelling and Length of Story (Number of Phrases) for Mother and Child

Reported Goals	Comprehension	Social	t
Mother			
n	9	25	
M (phrases)	102.44	157.76	2.42 ★
SD	41.37	68.03	
Child			
n	9	25	
M (phrases)	19.86	28.74	2.04 ★
SD	10.57	10.18	

★ *p* < .05

Due to limited sample size, only qualitative comparisons could be made between reported goals/styles and actual storytelling patterns. All mothers in the motive/cause group reported social enjoyment as their goal, compared to 78% in the story-event group and 50% in the non-interactive group. Similarly, 93% of mothers in the motive/cause group reported a preference for frequent questioning, versus 71% in the story-event group and 43% in the non-interactive group.

These findings indicate consistency between mothers' reported goals and styles and their observed storytelling behavior. Moreover, they suggest a link between maternal goals and children's verbal participation. Children whose mothers preferred active engagement showed higher levels of narrative contribution. Conversely, children whose mothers favored uninterrupted reading were generally less verbally responsive. These differing approaches appear to shape children's perception of reading—either as a participatory or receptive activity.

Further analysis explored how storytelling goals influenced the use of evaluatives. A two (goal) by four (evaluative type) mixed ANOVA revealed that mothers emphasizing comprehension used more character speech and goal-related evaluatives, while those emphasizing enjoyment used more meta-cognitive references (e.g., "What do you think will happen?"), $F(3, 132) = 4.22, p < .01$.

Children's evaluative use showed a similar pattern. Another mixed ANOVA revealed a main effect of evaluative type, $F(3, 132) = 7.83$, $p < .001$, and of maternal goal, $F(1, 132) = 4.37, p < .05$. Children whose mothers emphasized enjoyment used a higher proportion of evaluatives (M = 5.59, SD = 3) compared to those whose mothers emphasized comprehension (M = 3.39, SD = 3) (see Table 10).

Table 10

Mothers' Reported Goals of Storytelling and Mean Frequency (SD) of Evaluatives during Storytelling for Mother and Child

Evaluatives	Mothers' Goal: Comprehension	Mothers' Goal: Social Enjoyment
Mothers		
Frame of mind	5.57 (3.1)	6.14 (3.2)
Character speech	10.00 (10.2)	4.18 (3.5)
Goal-oriented	18.29 (9.6)	12.86 (6.7)
Meta-cognitive	8.00 (8.3)	14.21 (9.8)
Children		
Frame of mind	0.57 (1.5)	3.36 (3.5)
Character speech	1.29 (3.4)	2.75 (3.0)
Goal-oriented	7.00 (7.9)	9.00 (5.6)
Meta-cognitive	4.71 (6.9)	7.25 (7.2)

Together, these results suggest that maternal goals, shaped by educational background, influence both maternal and child narrative behaviors. We now turn to how these storytelling patterns relate to children's independent narrative performance.

Relationship Between Storytelling Pattern and Children's Independent Narratives

Do mother-child storytelling styles predict children's ability to narrate a story independently? To assess this, children's narratives were evaluated for structural coherence, defined by inclusion and correct sequencing of setting, initiating event, internal response, attempt, resolution, and outcome. The number of deviations from this prototypical structure served as the dependent variable.

Although small sample size limited statistical analysis by group, qualitative comparisons revealed marked differences. All children in the non-interactive group required prompting to generate a narrative, compared to 57% in the story-event group and 35% in the motive/cause group. This suggests that children in the motive/cause group were more likely to generate coherent narratives with minimal support.

A three (storytelling pattern) by two (child gender) by two (maternal education) mixed ANOVA showed a significant main effect for storytelling pattern, $F(2, 20) = 4.40$, $p < .026$, and an interaction between gender and education, $F(1, 20) = 8.33$, $p < .009$. Post-hoc comparisons revealed that children in the story-event ($M = 2.43$, $SD = 1.83$) and motive/cause groups ($M = 2.0$, $SD = 0.96$) made fewer structural deviations than those in the non-interactive group ($M = 5.25$, $SD = 1.0$) (see Table 11).

Regarding the gender by education interaction, female children with more educated mothers produced significantly more coherent narratives ($M = 2.0$, $SD = 1.10$) than those with less educated mothers ($M = 4.0$, $SD = 1.77$). No such differences were observed among male children. This finding suggests that maternal education may have a differential impact on daughters' narrative skills—perhaps influenced by the gender of the female experimenter conducting the post-reading interview. However, this remains speculative.

In sum, the data indicate that interactive storytelling, particularly when involving motive or causal reasoning supports children's narrative development. Non-interactive patterns may foster other skills (e.g., vocabulary or passive comprehension), but may not support independent storytelling to the same extent. These functional distinctions merit further investigation.

Children's Narrative Components and the Role of Evaluation

Prior research on young children's storytelling (e.g., Haslett, 1986; Miller & Sperry, 1981; Stein, 1988) has shown that children aged four to five often include core narrative components such as the initiating event, attempts, and outcomes, but frequently omit the setting and resolution. These patterns were evident in the current study. Most children independently narrated either the initiating event (e.g., "the frog escapes") or the internal response (e.g., "the frog is gone"), though initiating events were more prevalent (81%) than internal responses (55%). Approximately 36% of the children included both elements. Notably, all but one of the children who included both initiating event and internal response came from either the story-event or motive/cause storytelling groups.

Attempts to recover the frog and the eventual outcome (finding the frog) appeared in 75% of the narratives, but the setting (e.g., "the frog is in the jar") and resolution (e.g., "they take the frog home") were less frequently included—only 36% and 47%, respectively. These results align with earlier findings suggesting that young children are still developing the ability to narrate these less prominent elements. While most children appear able to construct a core narrative, the inclusion of settings, internal responses, and resolutions seems to emerge more gradually.

Among children in the motive/cause group, 87% constructed a core narrative, and 79% included a resolution. Fewer included the setting (36%) or internal response (43%). In the story-event group, the same percentage (87%) provided a core narrative, but more included the setting (57%) and internal response (64%), with fewer narrating the resolution (36%) (see Table 12). However, story elements in this group were often recounted out of chronological order—for example, mentioning the outcome before the initiating event. In contrast, children in the motive/cause group were more likely to place story components in appropriate temporal sequence.

Table 11

Children's Frequency (SD) of Deviation from a "Prototypic" Narrative Pattern According to Mother–Child Storytelling Pattern

Mother–Child Group	n	Deviation from Classic Pattern
Non-interactive	8	5.25 (1.00)
Story Event	14	2.43 (1.83)
Motive/Cause	14	2.00 (0.96)

Table 12

Children's Inclusion of Story Elements During Subsequent Storytelling According to Mother–Child Storytelling Pattern

Story Elements	Non-Interactive	Story Event	Motive/Cause
n	8	14	14
Core Elements★	2 (25%)	12 (87%)	12 (87%)
Setting	0	8 (57%)	5 (36%)
Internal Response	2 (25%)	9 (64%)	6 (43%)
Resolution	3 (36%)	5 (36%)	11 (79%)

Note: Initiating event, attempt, and outcome (consequence) represent a core narrative (Stein & Policastro, 1984).

Children in the non-interactive group were least likely to produce structurally coherent narratives. None of these children included the setting, and only three of the eight children included a resolution often incorrectly placed at the start of the narrative. Only two children in this group included an internal response, again often misordered. The majority failed to construct a core narrative. Only two children in this group successfully included the initiating event, attempt, and outcome in their independent retelling (see Table 12).

Evaluation During Joint Storytelling and Its Relationship to Independent Narration

To explore whether evaluation during joint storytelling was associated with children's ability to narrate specific story events, the use of four types of evaluatives (character speech, goal-oriented, internal state, and meta-cognitive) was analyzed across five story components: setting, initiating event, internal response, attempt/outcome, and resolution. Fisher exact tests revealed that meta-cognitive evaluations during narration of the setting ($p < .001$) and resolution ($p < .001$)

were significantly associated with children's inclusion of these components in their own independent stories.

Similarly, evaluative use of frame-of-mind (p < .001), character speech (p < .001), and goal-related reasoning (p < .001) during discussion of the resolution was also significantly associated with children's subsequent ability to narrate that part of the story. No significant associations were found for evaluative use during narration of the initiating event, internal response, or attempt/outcome.

These results suggest that evaluative commentary, particularly when applied to the setting and resolution, may support children's acquisition of these less frequently used narrative elements. Below are two illustrative examples, both drawn from children in the motive/cause group.

Example 1: Child Who Successfully Narrated the Setting

Joint Storytelling

M: "O.K. Now what's happened here?"
M: "The little puppy's looking at the frog."
C: "How come?"
M: "He's looking inside the [jar]."
C: "Jar."
M: "And they're both looking at the frog."
M: "I guess they like the frog."
M: "And it's nighttime."
M: "You can see the moon."
C: "Where? I don't see."
M: "Up in the window in the little boy's room."
C: "Oh yeah."
M: "And the little boy went sound asleep."

In this exchange, the child prompted the mother's explanation of the characters' motives (line 3), suggesting an emerging awareness of character intentions. This child later included a setting in their independent narrative:

Independent Narrative

C: *"Well, there is a little boy."*
E: *"Yeah?"*
C: *"And he had a frog."*
E: *"He had a frog?"*
C: *"And when he was sleeping the window was open a little bit…"*

Though less elaborate than the shared storytelling, this narration introduced the characters and their relationship (lines 1 and 3), indicating developmental progress in narrative coherence.

Example 2: Child Who Did Not Include the Setting

Joint Storytelling

M: *"What's happening in this picture?"*
C: *"The dog's looking at the frog in the bowl."*
M: *"The dog is looking at the frog in the bowl?"*
C: *"Yeah."*
M: *"Yeah."*
C: *"And the boy sitting [inaudible]."*
M: *"Yeah, alright. What time of day is it?"*
C: *"Night."*
M: *"How can you tell it's nighttime?"*
C: *"The moon's out."*
M: *"Well, that's a good thing."*
M: *"I didn't think about that."*
M: *"The moon is out. O.K."*

Here, the conversation lacked evaluative reflection on character intentions or relationships. The mother only evaluated the child's ability to infer time of day. This child did not include a setting in the subsequent narrative.

Evaluation During Narration of the Resolution

Two additional examples demonstrate how evaluation during the resolution phase of joint storytelling relates to children's narrative output.

Example 3: Child Who Included the Resolution

Joint Storytelling

M: *"He wanted to be with his friend."*
M: *"And a baby frog."*
M: *"And have a whole family."*
M: *"And what's this?"*
M: *"He has a new frog he's gonna take home with him."*
M: *"One of the babies."*
M: *"Bye bye, I'm gonna borrow your baby and leave this one."*
M: *"And then I'll bring it back."*
C: *"O.K."*
M: *"You think... you think when this one's grown up he'll bring it back to the pond to live?"*
M: *"There?"*
C: *"Mommy, I think he belongs there."*

In this instance, the mother invited evaluative thinking about the resolution, and the child responded reflectively. In her independent retelling, the child included the resolution:

Independent Narrative

C: *"And they found him."*
C: *"And then they went home again."*

Example 4: Child Who Did Not Include the Resolution

Joint Storytelling

M: *"You know what? They decided to give him a little frog."*
M: *"He gets to take one of the babies home."*
M: *"And the big frog is gonna stay home and take care of the family 'cause he's the daddy frog."*
M: *"Did you notice that?"*
M: *"And look—what is the boy doing in this picture?"*
C: *"Waving."*
M: *"He's waving goodbye."*
M: *"What do you think he's saying?"*
M: *"He's not saying, 'Frog, where are you?' anymore, is he?"*

C: "No."
M: "What's he saying?"
C: "I don't know."
M: "Saying: 'Thank you. I'll see you soon.'"
M: "'I will take good care of your baby.'"
M: "'Bye bye everybody.'"
M: "O.K. wasn't that a wonderful story?"
C: "Yeah."
M: "What happened—see, this was the end."
M: "There's no more pages."
M: "So tell me what happened on this last page?"
C: "He found all the frog."
M: "He found all the frogs."
M: "And he took which frog home?"
C: "The one baby."
M: "One of the babies?"
M: "Wasn't that a great story?"

Although the mother posed several questions, most were descriptive or tag questions. The child offered brief, unelaborated responses and ultimately narrated only the outcome—not the resolution.

This child had previously demonstrated an ability to narrate core elements and engage in some evaluative thinking, suggesting he was on the cusp of acquiring resolution skills. However, the mother's lack of high-level, evaluative questions during this part of the story may have limited his opportunity to practice and express this skill.

These examples suggest that evaluative engagement particularly during key moments such as the setting and resolution may play a pivotal role in supporting children's emerging narrative competence.

CONCLUSION

The results of this study corroborate prior research indicating differences in storytelling patterns between adults and children (Dickinson & Keebler, 1989; Pellegrini et al., 1990; Reese et al., 2010; Sobel & Letourneau, 2018; Hadley & Dickinson, 2021; Cleveland & Reese, 2021; Göncü & Tuerk, 2023; Maier et al., 2024). The current study delineated three distinct patterns: a non-interactive style characterized by passive listening, analogous to Dickinson and Keebler's "performance style" and Pellegrini's "low mental demand style"; a story-event-focused style involving maternal prompts regarding story events, comparable to the "interactive text-focused style" and "medium mental demand style"; and a motive/cause-focused style that fosters evaluative reasoning, resembling the "interactive conversational emphasis style" and "high mental demand style." Conversely, unlike Pellegrini's findings, the youngsters in the present study exhibited greater active participation.

It is essential to recognize the methodological differences among studies. This study employed a wordless picture book, unlike Pellegrini et al. (1990) and Dickinson & Keebler (1989), who utilized written texts. Pellegrini et al. found that the type of story affects how many and how good storytelling exchanges there are. The results here are almost the same as those of earlier research, even though there is no text.

Many of the moms who participated stated they had never read wordless books prior, which may have influenced their storytelling methods. As there was no written text, mothers may have focused more on making a story that made sense, which would have made it less interactive, even if they said their conduct was normal for how they usually read. Research by Rowe (2012), Zauche et al. (2016), and Wu & Billings (2023) confirms the hypothesis that the quality of parent-child interactions during reading sessions, rather than the sheer presence of text, predicts children's narrative outcome.

Additionally, the nonverbal responses of children (e.g., nodding) to yes/no and tag questions may not have been comprehensively recorded due to the lack of video documentation. Subsequent study should utilize video studies to elucidate the interaction between verbal and nonverbal storytelling approaches in both text-based and non-text literature.

All of the mothers read the identical picture book with no words, but they each recounted the story in their own way, based on their goals and what style they enjoyed most. These findings align with previous research linking storytelling style to reading proficiency (Heath & Thomas, 1984) and parental intention (Dickinson & Keebler, 1989). In this study, mothers selected narrative goals from six categories later collapsed into two groups: social enjoyment/enchantment and comprehension/school preparedness. While no mothers chose "other," categories, the structure of the question may have affected their answers.

Moms who wanted their kids to be ready for school and understand often didn't let them talk. Instead, mothers talked about what the story was about and what they believed the characters would say. These moms didn't talk to their kids about how the characters felt or ask them what they thought very often. Conversely, mothers prioritizing socialization and enjoyment facilitated discussions of the narrative by frequently referencing their own and their child's perspectives. Studies by Melzi and Caspe (2021), Reese et al. (2022), Reese & Newcombe (2007), and Tare et al. (2024) support this assertion, demonstrating that elaborative maternal strategies correlate with improved storytelling abilities and lasting academic benefits.

These sentiments were linked to mother's education. Mothers with less than 16 years of schooling were more likely to make sure their kids were ready for school and understood what they were being taught; while mothers with more education were more inclined to appreciate narratives featuring social interaction. The current sample had a higher level of educational attainment compared to prior studies on socioeconomic status (SES) and literacy, suggesting it may not be directly comparable to low-SES samples (Anderson, Teale, & Estrada, 1980; Heath, 1983; Hicks, 1991).

It also appeared that the mother's educational attainment influenced the child's level of participation. Mothers with higher levels of education were more inclined to motivate their children to narrate stories and reported reading with them daily. As a result, children whose mothers delineated interaction objectives participated more frequently and generated more intricate narratives. Haden et al. (2009), Hedrick & Winsler (2010), Tessler & Nelson (1994), and Lambert et al. (2023) have demonstrated analogous correlations between maternal assistance in children's learning and the complexity of their language and narratives.

Several mothers who told stories without their children said that their goals were to help their children understand and get ready for school. Still, the particular stories about their child were shorter in length and had more clear structural differences from standard story structures. This corroborates the findings of Demir-Lira et al. (2019), that moms who prioritize mental-state language and narrative assessment predicts their children's future storytelling capabilities and aligns with Sabbagh and Callanan (1998) who found that the way parents tell stories influences on how kids remember things and think.

These distinct techniques of delivering stories show that people have different ideas about what stories are for. Some educational settings tell students to "sit and listen," which makes it sound like they shouldn't do anything else. Parents could see storytelling as a way to convey information rather than as a way to connect with their child. On the other side, post high school often focuses on having significant conversations, looking at things from many points of view, and putting together a story. Mothers who have more education may be more likely to encourage participatory storytelling that includes children's points of view and helps them think critically to prepare them for higher level of education.

The data shows this. Mothers who were more educated had more books at home, reported they read more regularly, and considered that reading was a significant component of their family's social life. and their children were better at telling stories. Interactive storytelling goals and methods might give kids a lot of chances to make sense of things and share how they feel (Wertsch, 1985a, 1985b; Giraldo & Cooper, 2025). On the other hand, methods that put understanding first may make people less interested in how their brains and words work.

Kids who were told to think about what happened in the story did better on narrative tasks later than kids who weren't prompted. This aligns with the studies conducted by Haslett (1986), Miller and Sperry (1981), and Umiker-Sebeok (1979), which demonstrate that the utilization of evaluative language is crucial for narrative competence. Demir et al. (2015) shown that when parents utilize mental-state language and narrative structuring, it facilitates children's ability to narrate stories independently with emotional and causal coherence.

These results may have implications for pedagogical strategies. Kids who hear interactive stories at home might do better in class when it comes to talking about things, like asking questions and going into more detail. People who have never engage in interactive stories before may have problems later in school and in later life when these skills are required. It is essential to do research to analyze the impact of household narrative patterns on academic achievement in educational settings. Skarakis-Doyle & Dempsey (2008) and new longitudinal findings from Gutierrez & McCoy (2024) illustrate that children from more affluent narrative contexts benefit in literacy transitions and metacognitive awareness.

There were also differences between boys and girls. The narrative goals of parents were uniform irrespective of the child's gender; however, the actual interaction patterns exhibited variability, especially among moms possessing higher education levels. These moms seemed to ask various questions depending on how well their child told stories. For example, mothers asked their daughters less hard questions when they told stories on their own. Girls whose mothers had more education did better in narrative structure than girls whose moms had less education. On the other hand, boys whose mothers had less education did a little better than girls whose moms had more education, which shows that moms know and adapt to their kids' strengths.

It is also important to think about how the gender of the individual who did the experiment might have impacted the results. The female experimenter may have inadvertently selected female subjects instead of male ones. However, differences in storytelling style based on gender and maternal education imply that child performance cannot be exclusively ascribed to this factor.

Every parent who completed the study said that they read to their kids often and that they were the main reader, not the dad. This could help us understand why boys and girls tell stories in different ways. Future research ought to examine narrative consequences in households where fathers serve as the principal readers.

In conclusion, mothers' educational background, goals, and reading style not only related to child's gender but ultimately influenced mother-child storytelling. This study underscores the need of understanding the development and justification of both interactive and non-interactive parenting styles, which may be exhibited by all parents over time. We need more longitudinal studies to examine the developmental trajectory of cooperative storytelling and the impact on children's narrative skills. Finally, we need more research to examine how children's narrative choices and competencies affect these interactions.

REFERENCES

Applebee, A. N. (1978). *Child's concept of a story: Ages two to seventeen*. University of Chicago Press.

Ausubel, N. (1980). *A treasury of Jewish folklore* (Bantam abridged ed.). Bantam.

Bamberg, M. (1987). *The acquisition of narratives*. Mouton de Gruyter.

Bamberg, M. (2004). *Form and functions of narrative models. Narrative Inquiry, 14*(1), 1–17.

Bamberg, M., & Damrad, R. (in press). On the ability to provide evaluative comments: Further explorations of children's narrative competencies.

Bamberg, M., & Marchman, V. (1990). What holds a narrative together? The linguistic encoding of episode boundaries. *Papers in Pragmatics, 4,* 58-121.

Bettelheim, B. (1977). *The uses of enchantment: The meaning and importance of fairy tales.* Vintage Books.

Bohanek, J. G., Marin, K. A., Fivush, R., & Duke, M. P. (2006). *Family narrative interaction and children's sense of self. Family Process, 45(1), 39–54.*

Bork, H. (1971). Interpersonal perception of young children: Egocentrism or empathy. *Developmental Psychology, 5*(2), 263–269.

Botvin, G. J., & Sutton-Smith, B. (1977). The development of structural complexity in children's fantasy narratives. *Developmental Psychology, 13*(4), 377–388.

Bredart-Compernol, C., Rondal, J. A., & Peree, F. (1981). More about maternal and paternal speech to language learning children in various dyadic and triadic situational contexts. *International Journal of Psycholinguistics, 8*(4), 149–168.

Bretherton, I., & Beeghly, M. (1982). Talking about internal states: Acquisition of an explicit theory of mind. *Developmental Psychology, 18*(6), 906–921.

Bretherton, I., Fritz, J., Zahn-Waxler, C., & Ridgeway, D. (1986). Learning to talk about emotions: A functionalist perspective. *Child Development, 57*, 529–548.

Bruner, J. S. (1981) Concepts of the Child in Freud, Piaget, and Vygotsky. American Psychological Association Invited address, Los Angeles. In *Abstracts of 1981 Convention of the APA.*

Bruner, J. (1991). *The narrative construction of reality. Critical Inquiry*, 18(1), 1–21.

Bullock, M., & Russell, J. A. (1984). Preschool children's interpretation of facial expressions of emotions. *International Journal of Behavioral Development.*

Curenton, S. M., & Craig, M. J. (2011). *Shared-reading versus oral storytelling: Associations with preschoolers' vocabulary, comprehension, and narrative skills. Early Child Development and Care, 181*(1), 79–93.

Curenton, S. M., Craig, M. J., & Flanigan, N. (2020). Racial identity, family storytelling, and the development of African American children's academic skills. *Journal of Applied Developmental Psychology, 68*, 101144.

Damrad, R., & Bamberg, M. (1989, April). Form and function of evaluative language in narration. Paper presented at the Society for Research in Child Development, Kansas City, MO.

van Dijk, T. A. (1980). *Macrostructures*. Lawrence Erlbaum Associates.

de Beaugrande, R., & Colby, B. (1979). Narrative models of action and interaction. *Cognitive Science, 3*, 43–66.

Demir, Ö. E., Levine, S. C., & Goldin-Meadow, S. (2015). *Narrative skills in children with early brain injury: Can gesture help? Developmental Psychology, 51*(7), 811–825.

Demir, Ö. E., Rowe, M. L., Heller, G., Goldin-Meadow, S., & Levine, S. C. (2015). Narrative and mental state input predict theory of mind and narrative competence in preschoolers. *Journal of Child Language, 42*(3), 662–687. https://doi.org/10.1017/S0305000914000230

Dickinson, D., & Keebler, R. (1989). Variation in preschool teachers' styles of reading books. *Discourse Processes, 12*, 353–375.

Dyer, M. G. (1983). Role of affect in narratives. *Cognitive Science, 7*, 211–242.

Fivush, R., & Nelson, K. (2006). Parent–child reminiscing locates the self in the past. *British Journal of Developmental Psychology, 24*(1), 235–251.

Fivush, R., & Zaman, W. (2014). *Gender, subjectivity, and the development of autobiographical self. Advances in Child Development and Behavior, 46, 1–41.*

Georgakopoulou, A. (2007). *Small stories, interaction and identities*. John Benjamins.

Geva, E., & Olson, D. (1983). Children's story-retelling. *Discourse Processes, 4*, 85–110.

Glenn, C. G. (1978). The role of episodic structure and of story length in children's recall of simple stories. *Journal of Verbal Learning and Verbal Behavior, 17*, 229–247.

Guinagh, B. J., & Jester, R. E. (1972). How parents read to children. *Theory Into Practice, 11*(3), 171–177.

Habermas, T., & de Silveira, C. (2008). The development of global coherence in life narratives across adolescence: Temporal, causal, and thematic aspects. *Developmental Psychology, 44*(3), 707–721.

Haden, C. A., Haight, J. C., & Elischberger, H. B. (2009). Parent–child reminiscing and the construction of a subjective self. In J. M. Reese & M. Fivush (Eds.), *The development of autobiographical memory: Social and cultural perspectives* (pp. 162–183). Cambridge University Press.

Hammack, P. L. (2011). *Narrative and the politics of meaning. Narrative Inquiry, 21(2), 311–318.*

Harkins, D. A., & Michel, G. F. (submitted). Maternal storytelling influences on narrative skill of five-year-old children.

Harkins, D. A., & Michel, G. F. (1991, April). Adults adjust storytelling pattern according to whether the audience will be a child or an adult. Poster presented at the Society for Research in Adult Development, Boston, MA.

Harter, S. (1979, May). Children's understanding of multiple emotions: A cognitive-developmental approach. Address at the Ninth Annual Piaget Society Meeting, Philadelphia, PA.

Haslett, B. (1986). A developmental analysis of children's narratives. In D. G. Ellis & W. A. Donahue (Eds.), *Contemporary issues in language and discourse processes* (pp. 79–96). Lawrence Erlbaum Associates.

Hayden, H. M., & Fagan, W. T. (1983). Clarification strategies in joint book reading. *Discourse Processes, 4*, 131–142.

Heath, S. B. (1986). Taking a cross-cultural look at narratives. *Topics in Language Disorders, 7*(1), 84–94.

Hudson, J., & Nelson, K. (1983). Effects of script structure on children's story recall. *Developmental Psychology, 19*(4), 625–635.

Kemper, S. (1984). Development of narrative skills: Explanations and entertainments. In S. A. Kuczaj (Ed.), *Discourse development: Progress in cognitive developmental research* (pp. 99–122). Springer-Verlag.

Labov, W., & Waletzky, J. (1967). Narrative analysis: Oral versions of personal experience. In J. Helm (Ed.), *Essays on the verbal and visual arts* (pp. 12–44). University of Washington Press.

Lemish, D., & Rice, M. L. (1986). Television as a talking picture book: A prop for language acquisition. *Journal of Child Language, 13*, 251–274.

Lévi-Strauss, C. (1955). The structural study of myth. In T. A. Sebeok (Ed.), *Myth: A symposium* (pp. 81–106). Indiana University Press.

Lindholm, L. A., & Dockrell, J. E. (2012). *The narrative skills of children with SLI: A meta-analysis. Journal of Speech, Language, and Hearing Research, 55*(3), 714–729.

Maranda, P., & Maranda, E. K. (1971). *Structural models in folklore and transformational essays.* Mouton.

Mason, J. M., & Allen, J. (1982). A review of emergent literacy with implications for research and practice in reading. *Merrill-Palmer Quarterly, 28*(4), 471–484.

Mayer, M. (1969). *Frog, where are you?* Dial Press.

McAdams, D. P. (2008). *The life story interview. Northwestern University.*

McCabe, A., & Bliss, L. S. (2003). *Patterns of narrative discourse: A multicultural, life span approach.*

McLean, K. C., & Pasupathi, M. (2012*). Processes of identity development: Where I am and how I got there. Identity: An International Journal of Theory and Research, 12(1), 8–28.*

McNamee, G. D. (1979). Social interaction origins of narrative skills. *Quarterly Newsletter of the Laboratory of Comparative Human Cognition, 1*(4), 63–68.

Melzi, G., Schick, A. R., & Bostwick, E. (2013). Cultural variations in maternal narrative elaboration: Lessons from Latino families. *Journal of Cognition and Development*, 14(4), 486–510. https://doi.org/10.1080/15248372.2012.689387

Melzi, G., Schick, A. R., & Kennedy, J. L. (2011). Narrative elaboration and vocabulary development in Latino preschoolers. *Early Childhood Research Quarterly, 26*(4), 456–467.

Miller, P., & Sperry, L. (1988). Early talk about the past: The origins of conversational stories of personal experience. *Journal of Child Language, 15*(2), 293–315.

Miller, P. J., & Sperry, D. E. (2012). Déjà vu: The continuing misrecognition of low-income children's verbal abilities. *Social Policy Report, 26*(4), 1–17.

Nezworski, T., Stein, N. L., & Trabasso, T. (1982). Story structure versus content in children's recall. *Journal of Verbal Learning and Verbal Behavior, 21*, 196–206.

Ninio, A. (1983). Joint book reading as a multiple vocabulary acquisition device. *Developmental Psychology, 19*(3), 445–451.

Ninio, A., & Bruner, J. (1978). The achievement and antecedents of labeling. *Journal of Child Language, 5*, 5–15.

Paris, S. G., & Paris, A. H. (2003). *Assessing narrative comprehension in young children. Reading Research Quarterly, 38*(1), 36–76.

Pellegrini, A. D., Brody, G. H., & Siegel, I. (1985a). Parents' book-reading habits with their children. *Journal of Educational Psychology, 77*(3), 332–340.

Pellegrini, A. D., Brody, G. H., & Siegel, I. (1985b). Parents' teaching strategies with their children. *Journal of Psycholinguistic Research, 14*(6), 509–521.

Pellegrini, A. D., & Galda, L. (1990). The joint construction of stories by preschool children and an experimenter. In B. K. Britton & A. D. Pellegrini (Eds.), *Narrative thought and narrative language* (pp. 113–140). Lawrence Erlbaum Associates.

Pellegrini, A. D., Perlmutter, J. C., Galda, L., & Brody, G. H. (1991). Joint reading between black Head Start children and their mothers. *Child Development, 61*(2), 443–453.

Pennebaker, J. W., & Smyth, J. M. (2016). *Opening up by writing it down: How expressive writing improves health and eases emotional pain (3rd ed.).* Guilford Press.

Peterson, C., & McCabe, A. (1983). *Developmental psycholinguistics: Three ways of looking at a child's narrative.* Plenum Press.

Phillips, J. R. (1973). Syntax and vocabulary of mother's speech to young children: Age and sex comparisons. *Child Development, 44,* 182–185.

Poulson, D., Kintsch, E., Kintsch, W., & Premack, D. (1979). Children's comprehension and memory for stories. *Journal of Experimental Child Psychology, 28,* 379–403.

Pratt, M. W., Robins, S., Kerig, P., Cowan, P., & Cowan, C. P. (1989, April). Apprentice narrators: Parents as listeners and young children's acquisition of storytelling skills. Paper presented at the Society for Research in Child Development, Kansas City, MO.

Prince, G. (1973). *A grammar for stories.* Mouton.

Propp, V. (1958). *Morphology of the folktale.* University of Texas Press.

Quasthoff, U., & Nikolaus, K. (1981, September). What makes a good story. Paper presented at the International Symposium on Text Process, Freiburg, Switzerland.

Quasthoff, U. M. (1989, April). On the development of narrative discourse patterns: An explanatory approach. Poster presented at the Society for Research in Child Development, Kansas City, MO.

Reese, E., Haden, C. A., & Fivush, R. (1993). Parental styles of talking about the past. *Developmental Psychology, 29*(3), 596–606.

Reese, E., Leyva, D., Sparks, A., & Grolnick, W. (2010). Maternal elaborative reminiscing increases low-income children's narrative skills relative to dialogic reading. *Early Education and Development, 21*(3), 318–342.

Reese, E., & Newcombe, R. (2007). *Training mothers in elaborative reminiscing enhances children's autobiographical memory and narrative. Child Development, 78(4), 1153–1170.*

Rogoff, B. (in preparation). Social interaction as apprenticeship in thinking: Guided participation in spatial planning.

Rogoff, B., & Mistry, J. (1990). The social and functional context of children's remembering. In R. Fivush, J. Hudson, & U. Neisser (Eds.), *Knowing and remembering in young children.* Cambridge University Press.

Rogoff, B., Mosier, C., Mistry, J., & Goncu, A. (in press). Toddlers' guided participation in cultural activity. *Cultural Dynamics.*

Rogoff, B., & Wertsch, J. (Eds.). (1984). *Children's learning in the "zone of proximal development".* Jossey-Bass.

Sabbagh, M. A., & Callanan, M. A. (1998). Metacognition in mother–child conversations. *Cognitive Development*, 13(4), 541–560. https://doi.org/10.1016/S0885-2014(98)90019-1

Shapiro, L. R., & Hudson, J. A. (1989, April). Cohesion and coherence in preschool children's picture-elicited narratives. Paper presented at the Society for Research in Child Development, Kansas City, MO.

Skarakis-Doyle, E., & Dempsey, L. (2008). *Assessing story grammar elements in preschoolers' narratives: A study of typical development and language impairment. International Journal of Language & Communication Disorders,* 43(2), 133–153. https://doi.org/10.1080/13682820701261806

Smiley, P., & Huttenlocher, J. (1987). Early word meanings: The case of object names. *Cognitive Psychology, 19*(1), 63–89.

Snow, C. (1972). Mother's speech to children learning language. *Child Development, 43*, 549–566.

Sparks, A., & Reese, E. (2013). The benefits of reminiscing with young children. *Current Directions in Psychological Science, 22*(6), 400–405.

Sperry, D. E., Sperry, L. L., & Miller, P. J. (2019). Reexamining the verbal environments of children from different socioeconomic backgrounds. *Child Development, 90*(4), 1303–1318.

Stein, N. L. (1987). The development of children's storytelling skill. In M. B. Franklin & S. Barten (Eds.), *Child language: A book of readings* (pp. 282–297). Oxford University Press.

Stein, N. L., & Glenn, C. G. (1979, April). A developmental study of children's constructions of stories. Paper presented at the Society for Research in Child Development, New Orleans.

Stein, N. L., & Glenn, C. G. (1982). Children's concept of time: The development of a story schema. In W. Friedman (Ed.), *The developmental psychology of time* (pp. 255–282). Academic Press.

Stein, N. L., & Policastro, M. (1984). The concept of a story: A comparison between children's and teachers' viewpoints. In H. Mandl, N. L. Stein, & T. Trabasso (Eds.), *Learning and comprehension of text* (pp. 113–155). Lawrence Erlbaum Associates.

Stein, N. L., & Trabasso, T. (1989) Children's understanding of changing emotional states. In P. Harris & C. Saarni (Eds.), *The development of emotional understanding*. Cambridge University Press.

Suggate, S., Schaughency, E., McAnally, H., & Reese, E. (2018). *Parents' elaborative reminiscing styles and children's socioemotional and narrative development: A longitudinal study. Developmental Psychology*, 54(4), 659–673.

Sutton-Smith, B. (1975). The importance of the storyteller: An investigation of the imaginative life. *Urban Review, 8*, 82–95.

Tessler, M. H., & Nelson, K. (1994). Making stories: The role of parental prompts. *Journal of Narrative and Life History*, 4(2), 105–121.

Thorne, A., McLean, K. C., & Lawrence, A. M. (2004). *When remembering is not enough: Reflecting on* development in Latino preschoolers. *Early Childhood Research Quarterly, 26*(4), 456–467.

Toolan, M. J. (1988). *Narrative: A critical linguistic introduction*. Routledge.

Trabasso, T. R., Nickels, M., & Munger, M. P. (1989, November). Goals, plans, and actions in storytelling in pictures. Paper presented at the 30th Annual Meeting of the Psychonomic Society, Atlanta, GA.

Trabasso, T. R., Stein, N. L., & Johnson, N. S. (1981). Children's knowledge of events: A causal analysis of story structure. *Psychology of Learning and Motivation, 15*, 237–282.

Umiker-Sebeok, D. J. (1979). Preschool children's intraconversational narratives. *Journal of Child Language, 6*, 91–109.

Uzgiris, I. C., Benson, J. B., Kruper, J. C., & Vasek, M. E. (1989). Contextual influences on imitative interaction between mothers and infants. In J. J. Lockman & N. L. Hazen (Eds.), *Action in social context: Perspectives in early development* (pp. 215–230). Plenum.

Vygotsky, L. S. (1962). *Thought and language*. MIT Press.

Vygotsky, L. S. (1978). *Mind in society*. Harvard University Press.

Wertsch, J. V. (1985). *Culture, communication, and cognition: Vygotskian perspectives*. Cambridge University Press.

Wheeler, M. P. (1983). Context-related age changes in mothers' speech: Joint book reading. *Journal of Child Language, 10*, 259–263.

Yoder, P. J., & Kaiser, A. P. (1989). Alternative explanations for the relationship between maternal verbal interaction style and child language development. *Journal of Child Language, 16*, 141–160.

Yussen, S. R., Mathews, S. R., Buss, R. R., & Kane, P. T. (1980). Developmental change in judging important and critical elements of stories. *Developmental Psychology, 16*(3), 213–219.

Zaman, W., & Fivush, R. (2020). *Narrative coherence and identity: Associations in adolescence and emerging adulthood. Developmental Psychology, 56(3), 556–566.*

Zaman, W., & Fivush, R. (2020). Bridging the gap: Narrative coherence and children's developing sense of self. *Memory, 28*(3), 279–289.

Zauche, L. H., Thul, T. A., Mahoney, E. D., & Stapel-Wax, J. L. (2016). Language and literacy: Parent knowledge, attitudes, and practices. *Children and Youth Services Review*, 61, 66–72. https://doi.org/10.1016/j.childyouth.2015.12.017

APPENDIXES

Appendix A:
Mother–Child Storytelling Study – Sample Consent Form

Study Title: Narrative Development Through Joint Storytelling
Principal Investigator: [Insert Name]
Institution: [Insert University or Institution Name]
Contact: [Insert Email and/or Phone Number]

Purpose of the Study:

This study explores how young children and their caregivers co-construct stories while reading a wordless picture book together. The goal is to better understand the role of adult-child storytelling in early narrative development.

Procedures:
Participants will be asked to:

- Read a wordless picture book with their child during a video-recorded session.

- Answer a short set of questions regarding their typical storytelling habits and goals.

- Allow researchers to analyze the storytelling interaction and narrative content.

Risks and Benefits:

There are no foreseeable risks beyond those experienced in typical storytelling settings. Participants may gain insight into their storytelling styles and how they engage with their child.

Confidentiality:

All information collected will be kept confidential. Video recordings will be used solely for research purposes and stored securely.

Voluntary Participation:

Participation is voluntary. You may withdraw from the study at any point without penalty.

Consent:

By signing below, you consent to participate in the above-described research study.

Appendix B:
Questions to Be Asked During Recall

Free Recall Prompt

"Let's pretend your best friend is here, and they've never read this story" (pointing to the frog book) "that you read with your mom. Can you tell them what happens in the story?"

The storybook will be held in front of the child as a visual cue.

No additional verbal prompts (e.g., title or character names) will be provided.

Only minimal verbal encouragement will be offered (e.g., "yes," "uh-huh," "go on," "mm-hmm").

The child may continue narrating until one of the following occurs:

- They indicate they are finished.
- They state they cannot remember more.
- They pause for more than 2–3 minutes.

Probe Questions to Elicit Further Narration

If key story elements are missing during free recall, the experimenter may gently prompt with neutral questions or reframe the child's prior comments to encourage elaboration.

For example:

Child: "The boy looked in the hole."

Experimenter: "The boy looked in the hole?"

Targeted Prompts by Narrative Element

- Setting
  - Who was in the story?
  - What were they doing?
  - And then what?

- Initiating Event
  - What happened to the frog?
  - And then what?

- Internal Response
  - What did the boy do next?

- Attempts
  - What did the bees do?
  - What happened next?

- Outcomes / Consequences
  - (Continue narrative prompts based on child's engagement and prior responses.)

Ending Criteria

Probing will conclude if any of the following occur:

- 10 minutes have passed.
- The child pauses for more than 2–3 minutes.
- The child shows frustration or disinterest.

Appendix C:
Parent Interview Form

Child's Name:_____

Age:_____ 3. Date of Birth (DOB):_____

Date of Testing (DOT): _____

Daycare Attended (if any): _____

Siblings (Names & Ages): _____

Educational Level of:

Mother: _____

Father: _____

Who typically reads to your child?

How often?

Do you usually read alone to your child or with a sibling present?

Do you read differently to your child than your child's...
(Please circle Yes or No and describe how, if Yes)

Reader Yes / No   How?

Father Yes / No   _____

Grandmother Yes / No   _____

Grandfather   Yes / No   _____

Aunt   Yes / No   _____

Uncle Yes / No   _____

Teacher Yes / No   _____

Other Yes / No   _____

Please check all types of books read with your child:

☐ Picture books (no words)
☐ Storybooks with words
☐ Information books
☐ Chapter books
☐ Children's magazines
☐ Other: _____

Rank the following goals of storytelling in order of importance (1 = most important):

☐ My child comprehends the story
☐ A social time for relaxation and enjoyment
☐ To enchant my child with the "magic" of books
☐ Help my child prepare for school
☐ My child has reading readiness
☐ Other: _____

Please indicate how often you engage in the following activities when reading with your child:

Statement

Always	Frequently	Sometimes	Never
a. I read uninterrupted, only pausing to explain confusing parts			
☐	☐	☐	☐
b. I pause to ask questions to check understanding			
☐	☐	☐	☐
c. I frequently discuss pictures, characters, and story events			
☐	☐	☐	☐
d. I stop to talk about new vocabulary			
☐	☐	☐	☐

Which of the tapes did you prefer?

b. Why?

Do you ever read like Tape #1?
☐ Yes   ☐ No

b. When?

Do you ever read like Tape #2?

☐ Yes   ☐ No

b. When?

(e.g., emotional state, time of day, familiarity with story, story length)

How would you describe your role during storytelling?
(Select one)

☐ Too active—child not involved
☐ Very active—but necessary
☐ Active—but allowed child involvement
☐ Not too active or passive—just right
☐ Passive—but involved
☐ Very passive—but necessary
☐ Too passive—child not involved

How would you describe your child's role during storytelling?
(Select one)

☐ Very active and interested
☐ Very active and uninterested
☐ Active and interested
☐ Active and uninterested
☐ Passive and interested
☐ Passive and uninterested
☐ Very passive and interested
☐ Very passive and uninterested

Appendix D:
Comparison of Episodic (Bamberg, 1987) and Goal (Trabasso, 1992) Structure of Frog, Where Are You? by Mercer Mayer

Picture	Episodic Structure	Goal Structure
1	Major setting	Setting
2	Initial event	Initial event
3	Internal response	Internal response
4	Instantiation — Event 1 (IE)	Attempt 1 — Looking for frog
5	Continuation — Consequence 1	Attempt 2 — Calling for frog
6	Consequence 2	Goal failure
7	Consequence 3	Goal failure
8	Reinstantiation	Attempt 3 — Reinstatement of goal
9	Continuation — Event 2 (IE)	Attempt 4 — Look in hole
10	Consequence	Goal failure
11	Reinstantiation — Event 3 (IE)	Attempt 5 — Look in tree
12	Consequence	Goal failure → Outcome
13		Goal failure →
14	Reinstantiation — Event 4 (IE)	Attempt 6 — Calling for frog
15	Consequence 1	Goal failure
16	Consequence 2	" " →
17	Consequence 3	" " →
18	Consequence 4	Outcome
19	Reinstantiation — Event 5 (IE)	Initiating event — Boy hears frog
20	Continuation — Consequence 1	Subgoal — Tells dog to be quiet
21	Continuation — Consequence 2	Attempt 7 — Looks over log
22	Completion — Consequence 3	Successful outcome
23	Consequence 4	Outcome
24	Final response	Resolution

Appendix E:
Maternal Questions

- **A. Labeling Questions**
  e.g., "Who is this?" / "What is that?"

- **B. Yes/No Questions**
  e.g., "Is this a dog?" / "Did the boy do that?"

- **C. Tag Questions**
  e.g., "He's looking in the hole, isn't he?"

- **D. Text-related Links to Prior Experience**
  e.g., "Do you remember when you found a bee's nest?"

- **E. Descriptive-Event Questions**
  e.g., "What happened?" / "…then what?"

- **F. Evaluative Questions**
  e.g., "Why do you think he is looking over the log?"

Appendix F:
Evaluative Comments

- **Internal Cognitive and Affective States of Characters**
  e.g., "The boy is happy." / "Rover is surprised."
  (Includes terms like: sad, angry, afraid, surprised, curious, frustrated, thinking, wants, loves, etc.)

- **Character Speech**
  e.g., "The boy says: 'Frog, are you in there?'"
  e.g., "The owl said: 'Get out of my tree.'"

- **References to Absent Characters or Objects**
  e.g., "The jar is empty." / "The frog is gone." / "Frog, where are you?"

- **Meta-Cognitive Reflections**
  e.g., "I don't think the deer is going to like having a boy on his head."
  e.g., "What do you think the boy will do next?"

Appendix G:
Responses to Questions

- **A. Labeling**
  Q: "Who is that?" → *A:* "Doggy."

- **B. Verifying**
  Q: "Is he in the boot?" → *A:* "No."

- **C. Confirming**
  Q: "Those are antlers, huh?" → *A:* "Yeah."

- **D. Narrating Story Elements**
  Q: "What happened while he's in bed?" → *A:* "He's jumping out."

- **E. Explaining Motive or Cause**
  Q: "Why does the boy look like that?" → *A:* "Because he broke the jar."

- **F. Narrating Personal Experience**
  Q: "Do the bees sting him?" → *A:* "The bee tried to bite me."

Appendix H:
Coding for Child's Storytelling

- **Narrative Structure Codes**
  - **S** = Setting
  - **IE** = Initiating Event
  - **IR** = Internal Response
  - **A** = Attempt
  - **C** = Consequence
  - **R** = Reaction

- **Setting**: Mentions of boy/dog looking at frog, it's nighttime, moon, going to bed.

- **Initiating Event**: Frog escapes, jumps from jar.

- **Internal Response**: Frog is gone, escaped, or not there.

- **Attempt**: Looking/calling for frog (e.g., in boot, under bed, out window, in hole, over log, etc.).

- **Consequence**: Child finds the frog.

- **Reaction**: Child expresses happiness, takes frog home.

Appendix I:
Examples from three mother-child groups

Example from Low-Level Interactive Group

Case #26 – Female

Mother (M): *Frog, where are you?*
John and his dog Rover sat looking at the frog they had captured earlier this afternoon.
The frog was in the jar.
While John and Rover were sleeping, the frog sneaked out of the jar!

Child (C): *And he hopped out.*
Where um… in the name of God.
They had… I don't know where at.

M: *When they woke up, the jar was empty.*

C: *Yeah.*

M: *"Where did the frog go, Rover?"*
He picked up his boot and looked in his boot.
"Frog, are you in there?"
And Rover stuck his head in the jar.
And Rover got his head stuck in the jar.

C: *(laughs) I like that part.*

M: *John opened the window and yelled out, "Frog, where are you?"*
As John yelled, Rover fell out the window.
So John had to go outside and pick him up.
While they were outside, they decided to look for the frog.
John yelled, "Frog, where are you?"
All Rover did was watch the bees buzzing by his head.

C: *I hate…*

M: *John found a hole in the ground.*
So he yelled down the hole, "Frog, where are you?"

C: *(laughs)*

M: *"Where are you?"*
And Rover jumped up and down at the bees and the hive above his head.
Just then, a little groundhog came out and bit John right on the nose.
And then Rover got the bees very upset because he knocked down the bees'
nest.
John climbed up to a tree and looked inside the tree.

C: *Yeah.*

M: *An owl jumped out, which scared John and made him fall to the ground.*
And at the same time, the bees were chasing Rover because he knocked
down the hive.

C: *The hive, the bees' nest.*

M: *The bees' nest.*

C: *That?*

M: *That's a rock.*
John climbed up on top of a rock.

C: *And he was holding onto branches.*

M: *Let me finish the story (laughing).*
He held onto two branches that were at the top of the rock and yelled, "Frog,
where are you?"

C: *They were horns.*

M: *But they weren't branches.*
They were the antlers of a reindeer.

C: *They're horns.*

M: *Well, horns and antlers are the same thing.*
So when they…

C: *(unintelligible)*

M: *When the reindeer stood up, John was on top of his head, which got the*
reindeer mad.
So he ran.

And he ran right to the edge of a cliff and threw John off.
And Rover went with him.

C: *Do they die?*

M: *And they landed right in the water.*
When John sat up he said, "Listen, I hear something."

C: *(unintelligible)*

M: *(unintelligible) in the water.*
"Shh, I hear something over here behind this log. Let's see what it is."

C: *"Let's sneak up."*

M: *(laughs)*

C: *(laughs)*

M: *And there was Frog and his friend.*
And out around the corner came a bunch of baby frogs.
So John took a baby frog and waved bye to the big frog and said, "Bye, we'll see you again soon."
The end.

Child Retelling – Case #26

Experimenter (E): *Can you tell me the story?... (long pause)*

C: *A frog, where are you?*

E: *Alright, good job.*

C: *Froggie... (long pause)*

E: *Yeah, what else? (pause)*
Can you tell it to me like a story?

C: *I can.*

E: *You tell me the story.*

C: *I can't.*

E: *I bet you can. (pause)*

C: *I don't know how to read.*

E: *I bet you're a good storyteller.*

C: *I don't know how to read.*

E: *You don't have to read, you can just tell me about it, okay?*

C: *I can't…*

Example from story-event focused mother-child group

#38 Female

M: *O.K. The name of the book is Frog, where are you.*
and there's a little boy and his doggie and they
have a frog in their jar.

C: *Yeah.*

M: *and it's nighttime and the doggie and the little*
boy are looking at the frog.
What do you think the little boy's name is?

C: *I don't know.*
Is he Mack?

M: *Mack?*

C: *Yeah.*

M: *We can call him Mack*
and what's the doggy's name?

C: *Rupo*

M: *Rupo?*

C: *Yeah*

M: That's a funny name
  I like that.
  and what about the frog?

C: How about Tootoe?

M: Tootoe?

C: Yeah

M: O.K. but the little boys in his jamies
  and he's gonna go bed
  He goes to bed
  and the doggy winds up on the bed with him and
  they're sleeping.
  The frog climbed out of the jar.
  but it's morning time.
  and the sun comes in the window.
  and the little boy and the doggie wake up.
  and they look over the bed at the jar, empty.
  what happened?

C: The frog got out.

M: He went out.
  Ah, and they looked all over the room for him.
  He put his clothes on
  He looks in his boots.
  and they turn over the stool.
  and what's the dog doing?

C: He's getting in.

M: He's looking in the jar.
  and they open up the window.
  and they yell out the window "Tootoe, where are
  you?"
  Mack's calling him "Tootoe, where are you?"

C: "Tootoe, where are you?"

M: and what was the doggy's name again?

C: Rupo

M: Rupo?
  Ah, Rupo crawled out of the window.
  and Mack just looks at him
  and the dog breaks the froggy's jar.
  Poor Tootoe isn't going to have a home when they
  find him, is he?
  but the doggy's O.K.
  but Mack is pretty mad at Rupo, isn't he?

C: but you know where they can put him?
  He can hold him and put him in a cage.

M: put the foggy in a cage?

C: Yeah

M: Well maybe you could do that, sure.
  O.K. they go out into the field
  and Mack is calling Tootoe.

C: "Tootoe…"

M: "…Where are you?"

C: "…where are you?"

M: and and they Mack looking down at the hole.
  and then Rupo starts barking at some bees he sees
  in a tree.
  Oh what came out of the hole?

C: a beaver.

M: a beaver, maybe the beaver bit Mack's nose.

C: Yeah.

M: Ah.. Oh he was probably mad at him for looking in
  the hole, huh.

The dog starts barking at the bees
barking then looks what happens.
The hive falls down out of the tree and all the
bees start to swarm.
You don't want to have bees like that.
and the groundhog is just looking at Mack.
Well Mack climbs up into another tree to look at a
different hole.
He's still looking for Tootoe.

C: *Tootoe*

M: *"Tootoe, where are you?"*

C: *"Tootoe, where are you?"*

M: *but then the bees are chasing poor Rupo.*
"Run, Rupo. Don't let the bees get you."
Well look. what happenend to Mack?

C: *He fell down.*

M: *He fell down cause an owl scared him.*
came out of a hoe in a tree.

C: *Yeah.*

M: *My goodness, poor Mack, the owls mad at him.*
He's probably yelling at him, huh?
Well Mack decides to climb up the rock.
and he's calling

M: *what's he yelling?*

C: *"Tootoe, where are you?"*

M: *That's right.*
He's leaning on the branches.
The poor doggy's coming back because the bees got
him.
Do you think the bees would sting him?

C: Yeah.

M: Yeah, probably
   Ah, look what happenend to Mack.
   A deer picks him up, right on his head

C: Deer.

M: Those were antlers.
   Those weren't trees
   Oh, and the deer is running.
   Ah… Oh Mack, look out!
   He's still on his head
   and Rufro is barking and barking
   Ah and the deer throws Mack off the little cliff.
   and Rofro falls down too.
   and they fall right into some water.
   Oh… then look Roofroe climbs up on Mack's head.
   He doesn't want to get wet.
   He doesn't like the water I guess, huh?
   Now, Mack is saying: "Shh"
   "Roofroe, we have to find Tootoe."
   "Now you be quiet."
   and they look over a big tree stump near the pond
   ha look what they see
   a mommy froggy and a daddy froggy
   think daddy was Tootoe… was daddy?

C: Yeah

M: Isn't that nice?
   Oh and look all the little baby frogs that are
   there.
   and it's a nice happy family.
   Isn't that nice?
   Oop and the mommy froggy and Tootoe let Mack and
   Roofroe take home one of the baby froggies.
   so now Mack has a new froggy.
   Where's he gonna put him?

C: I don't know
He in a.. in a… he gonna put him in a cage.

M: It must be a cage huh.
cause what happened?
what did Roofroe do with the bottle?

C: He looked outside and he broke it

M: He broke it when he fell out the window, huh?

C: Yeah

M: Yeah

M: The End.

Child Retelling #38

C: I… I um the frog Tootoe

M: Tootoe

E: That's his name?

C: Yeah

E: Yeah what else?

C: Ah, I remembered um… the dog and the boy

E: Yeah

C: Yup, I remember the morning and the deer and the bees

E: The morning and the deer?

C: and the… and the… and the baby a frog.
and a… and a pouch
and a water

E: a pouch and a water?

C: Yeah

E: and what about the boy and the dog?

C: What?

E: What about them?

C: What?

E: what about the boy and the dog?

M: Tell her what happenend in the story?

C: I don't know

E: What was the story about?

C: The truth d.. Tootoe <can't understand>

M: What happenend to Tootoe?

C: He was lost

E: He was lost?

C: Yeah

E: and then what happenend?

C: He caught Tootoe.

E: They caught him.

C: Yeah

E: and then what happenend?

C: They called him.

M: They called him.

E: They called him?

C: Yeah And then it was the end

E: and that was the end

C: Yeah

E: They called him and that was the end?

C: Yeah and he picked a baby frog up

E: They picked a baby frog up

C: Yeah I'm gonna read it

Example from Motive/Cause Focused Mother-Child Group

Case #21 – Female

Mother (M): *This book is called* Frog, Where Are You? *by Mercer Mayer. See this little boy? He looks like he's calling out to somebody.*

Child (C): *Looks like he's saying, "Help, help, where is my frog?"*

M: *And what is the dog doing?*

C: *He's looking down to see if the dog is in the water.*

M: *You mean the frog in the water.*
Let's begin Frog, Where Are You? *by Mercer Mayer.*
It's nighttime—see the moon is outside.
And the little boy is looking down at his frog, and his little dog is looking at the frog in the jar.
See? Looks like he's taking off his clothes, and he's got his PJs on.
And he goes to sleep.
And the little dog curls up with him.
And look—the frog is climbing out of the jar.
And in the morning—see the sun is coming in the window.
Look honey, see the sun is coming in the window?

C: *I know.*

M: *And the little boy looks at the jar.*
He says, "Oh goodness, where has my frog gone?"
So he looks in his boot and turns his boot upside down.
And it looks like the doggy and somebody has turned the stool over and

checked under the stool.
And the little doggy has stuck his head in the jar to see if the froggy is in there.
The little boy is calling out the window.
What do you think he is calling?

C: *He's calling, "Froggy, where are you?"*

M: *Uh-huh. And the little dog has his head in the jar.*
And look—the doggy falls out the window.
And the little boy—oh goodness.
And the little boy looks—what does he… little boy look like he is now?

C: *Very angry.*

M: *Why is he angry?*

C: *Because the puppy…*

M: *Well, I don't know.*
I think that maybe—looks at his big boots.
He's got those big boots on.
I think that the jar is broken.
See, he fell out the window and the jar is all broken.
Now the little doggy is just looking at him saying, "It's okay."

M: *So they go off looking for the frog.*
The little boy is probably shouting, "Frog, where are you?"
And he looks down a hole and shouts, "Frog, where are you?"
And the little doggy—what's this hanging from the tree?

C: *A cone.*

M: *What do you think is inside?*

C: *Bees.*

M: *Yeah.*

C: *And honey.*

M: And the little doggy is more interested in the bees right now.
And he's shouting, "Woof, woof, woof."
And look at what comes out of the hole.
And the little boy looks like he is either holding his nose or doing something.
What is he doing?

C: He's saying, "Oh my gosh, it's smelly."

M: What do you think is smelly?

C: The skunk. (laughs)

M: Oh, do you think that's a skunk?
It might be. It's hard to tell.
Why is it hard to tell?

C: Because you can't see its tail.

M: Yeah, the tail is a pretty good sign of a skunk, isn't it?

C: Yeah.

M: It's striped—it's black and white-striped, isn't it?
Well, the little boy is still continuing his hunt.
So he goes up in the tree and he looks into the hole.
And the doggy is now astounded because the bee's hive has fallen out of the tree and all the bees are swarming.

C: What does swarming mean?

M: Well, it means they're all in a clump.
They're all gathering together.
Bees do that—they swarm.
They all get together in a big clump.
And they all travel together.
They all fly together in a big group.
And they're furious.
And look—they're following the doggy because their home has been knocked down.
And they've gone by so quickly that the little boy falls out of the tree.
And an owl pops out his head and says, "My goodness, what's happening?"

And the little boy looks like he... he's either hit his head and trying hard to put his hand over his head 'cause it hurts or—

M: Why does he look like that?

C: Because he, um... because he doesn't want the owl to land on his head.

M: Maybe. And he's on top of the rock and saying, "Where are you, frog? Frog, where are you?"
And the owl's gone back to his tree.
And the dog is sort of slinking around.
And then look—what happened?

C: He...

M: He was on top of a rock, holding onto what he thought was the branches of a tree.
But what were they?

C: Antlers.

M: Yeah, they were the deer's antlers.
And the deer lifts up his head and carries the boy off.
The dog thinks it's either great fun and very funny, or thinks he wants to have his little friend down.
He's running along next to the deer, barking.
But look where they are running—oh, they stop just before a cliff.
And the deer... the deer stops suddenly, and the boy falls off.
And so does the doggy—off this little cliff into something.
What do they fall off into?

C: The water.

M: Yeah, it's a pond and—SPLASH!

C: It's either a pond, a river, or mud water.

M: Uh-huh. And he falls off—KERPLUNK!—into the water, whatever kind of water it is.
And what's this? Do you know what that thing is called?

C: A lilypad.

M: Yeah, that's right—a lilypad, Lea.
And the little boy is just relieved not to be hurt.
And the little doggy climbs on his head.
And he has his hand up to his ear.
Why do you think he has... has his hand up to his ear?

C: Uh... to hear "Ribbit" or not.

M: Or to see if he hears the "Ribbit."

C: Yeah.

M: And he says, "Shh."
And he looks down and he looks over.
And what does he find?

C: Two froggies.

M: Yeah. Do you think one of these froggies is his?

C: No, I think one of these froggies is his.

M: One of the babies?

C: Yeah.

M: Really? Gee.
And he climbs over—oh goodness—and says, "Goodbye."
And he takes another little tiny frog home.
And look—he's got one there.
And that's either one of his frogs or one of the big frogs is.
And he's just taking another little one home.
That's the end of the story.
And you can see—that's kind of a large-looking frog when you see it in the jar.
So maybe his froggy has found... someone that he—another little froggy.
And they've had a family.
It's sort of hard to tell.
Maybe this one jumping is his frog—been visiting another family.
See? 'Cause there's one down there thinking, "Oh, how can I get back up?"
And that's the gap that's left behind.
See? It's hard to tell.
But that was a good story.

Child Retelling – Case #21

Child (C): *Inside the book... um... a little boy was sleeping... um...*
And while... um... little boy... um... and while the little boy was sleeping,
the frog climbed out of the jar. (laughs)
And then (laughs)—

Experimenter (E): *He did?*

C: *Yeah.*

E: *And what else?*

C: *And then... um... when the little boy woke up, then he... he couldn't*
find the frog.
And then... um... he climbed out... over a bridge.
And... um... and he thought... um... it was antlers to a deer was part of the branches.

E: *He did?*

C: *Yeah.*
And by mistake... um... he was on the deer.
And the deer... um... ran him to a river.
And the... the deer pushed... the little boy into... the river.

E: *He did?*

C: *Yeah.*
And then the frog... um... found... another frog.
And then... um... the little boy took the... um... another little frog.

E: *He did?*

C: *Yup.*

E: *He took another little frog?*

C: *Yup.*

E: *Anything else?*

C: No, that's it.

Appendix J:
Author Bibliography Key References

1985: Michel, G. F., & Harkins, D. A. Concordance of handedness between teacher and student facilitates learning manual skills. *Journal of Human Evolution, 14,* 597-601.

1986: Michel, G. F., & Harkins, D. A. Postural and lateral asymmetries in the ontogeny of handedness during infancy. *Developmental Psychobiology, 19,* 247-258.

Michel, G. F., Ovrut, M. R., & Harkins, D. A. Hand-use preferences for reaching and object manipulation in 6-13-month-old infants. *Genet Social General Psych Monographs, 111,* 407-428.

1987: Michel, G. F., & Harkins, D. A. Ontogenetic considerations in the phylogenetic history and adaptive significance of the bias in human handedness. *Behavior and Brain Sciences.*

1988: Harkins, D. A., & Michel, G. F. Evidence for maternal effect on infant hand-use preferences. *Developmental Psychobiology, 21,* 535-542.

1990: Michel, G. F., Harkins, D. A., & Meserve, A. Sex differences in neonatal state and head orientation. *Infant Behavior and Development, 13*(4), 461-467.

1991: Alexander, K., Michel, G. F., & Harkins, D. A. (April). Sex differences in parental influences on children's storytelling abilities. Seattle, WA. Presented at Society for Research Child Development.

Michel, G. F., Alexander, K., Case, D. E., Harkins, D. A., Kroonberg, P., & Rivera, M. (April). Maternal storytelling affects narrative skill of five-year-old children. Seattle, Washington. Presented at Biennial meeting of the Society for Research Child Development.

Harkins, D. A., & Uzgiris, I. C. Hand-use matching between mothers and infants during the first year. *Infant Behavior and Development, 14*(3), 289-298.

Harkins, D. A., & Michel, G. F. (July). Adults adjust storytelling patterns according to whether the audience will be a child or an adult.

Presented at Society for Research in Adult Development, Boston, MA. Society for Research in Adult Development.

1993: Harkins, D. A. Parental goals and styles of storytelling. In J. Demick, K. Bursik, & R. Dibiase (Eds.), *Parental Development*. NY: Taylor and Francis.

1994: Alexander, K. J., Harkins, D. A., & Michel, G. F. Sex differences in parental influences on children's storytelling skills. *Journal of Genetic Psychology, 155*(1), 47-58.

Harkins, D. A., Koch, P., & Michel, G. F. Listening to maternal storytelling affects narrative skill of 5-year-old children. *Journal of Genetic Psychology, 155*(2), 247-257.

1996: Harkins, D. A., & Ray, S. (August). Parent-child storytelling in Indian and American culture. Presented at XIV Biennial ISSBD, Quebec City, Canada. XIV Biennial ISSBD.

2001: Shulova, I., Logan, M., & Harkins, D. A. (October). Parent-child storytelling: Cultural differences among Russian immigrants and American parents. Danbury, CT. Presented at New England Psychological Association.

2002: Shulova, I., Logan, M., & Harkins, D. A. (March). Parent-child storytelling: Fact or fiction. Boston, MA. Presented at Eastern Psychological Association.

Donovan, N., Miller, V., & Harkins, D. A. (April). Searching for emotions: Age differences in mother-child storytelling. Presented at Conference of Human Development NC.

Logan, M., Shulova, I., & Harkins, D. A. (April). Where are we? Culture and gender differences in the expression of emotions during parent-child storytelling. Presented at Conference on Human Development NC, North Carolina.

2004: Harkins, D. A., Ray, S., Donovan, N., Miller, V. Mother-child storytelling styles across cultures, class and clinically depressed populations. Boston, MA. Presented at Suffolk University, ESL Annual Conference.

Harkins, D. A., Ray, S., Donovan, N., Miller, V., Shulova, I., & Logan, M. (May). Psychosocial variables and the narrative structure, style and content of parent-child storytelling. Boston, MA. Presented at Massachusetts Association of Teachers.

Harkins, D. A., & Ray, S. An exploratory analysis of mother-child storytelling in East India and Northeast North American cultures. *Narrative Inquiry, 14*(2), 347-367.

Shulova, I., Harkins, D. A., & Donovan, N. (February). Parental influence on narrative development of preschoolers. San Jose, CA. Presented at Society for Cross-Cultural Research.

2005: Shulova-Piryatinsky, I., & Harkins, D. A. (May). Cultural narratives: Exploratory study of mother-child storytelling in Russian and Northeast United States. Presented at Society for Cross-cultural Research, Santa Fe, NM.

2006: Miller, V., & Harkins, D. A. (May). When do mothers shelter and when do they warn: Age differences in mother-child storytelling. Wolfville, Nova Scotia. Presented at Narratives Matters Conference.

Piryatinsky, I., & Harkins, D. A. (May). Immigrant narratives: Exploratory study of mother-child storytelling in Russian immigrants in the US and Israel. Wolfville, Nova Scotia. Presented at Narrative Matters Conference.

Piryatinsky, I., & Harkins, D. A. (October). Cultural narratives of immigrant and non-immigrant mother-child storytelling. Presented at Boston College, Boston, MA. Diversity Challenge.

2007: Piryatinsky, I., & Harkins, D. A. (February). Catching the frog or letting it go: Narrative discourse of Russian Jewish immigrants in the United States and Israel. San Antonio, TX. Society for Cross-cultural Research.

2009: Piryatinsky, I., & Harkins, D. A. Exploratory study of narrative discourse: Russian immigrants' mother-child storytelling in Israel and Northeast United States. *Narrative Inquiry, 19*(2), 328-355.

2022: Harkins, D. A., & Miller, V. Age and gender differences in mother-child storytelling with preschool children. *Academia Letters*. https://doi.org/10.20935/AL5276

2025: Harkins, D. A., & Donovan, N. (in prep). Coping styles as ex-pressed through mother-child storytelling.

AUTHOR INDEX

www.ingramcontent.com/pod-product-compliance
Lightning Source LLC
Chambersburg PA
CBHW052142270326
41930CB00012B/2981